Some Bunny to Love

The Children's Rabbit Care Guide

Written by

Fiel John Meria

Some Bunny to Love
The Children's Rabbit Care Guide

Published in 2019 by St. Matthew's Publishing Corporation
(through its imprint Kahel Press)

ISBN 978-971-625-425-9

How to Order Purchase individual copies from www.stmatthews.ph

Copies are also available at special rates in bulk orders. Contact the publisher through the details below.

St. Matthew's Publishing Corporation First RVC Building, 92 Anonas Cor. K-6th Streets, East Kamias, Quezon City (02) 8426-5611 || inquiry@stmatthews.ph || www.stmatthews.ph

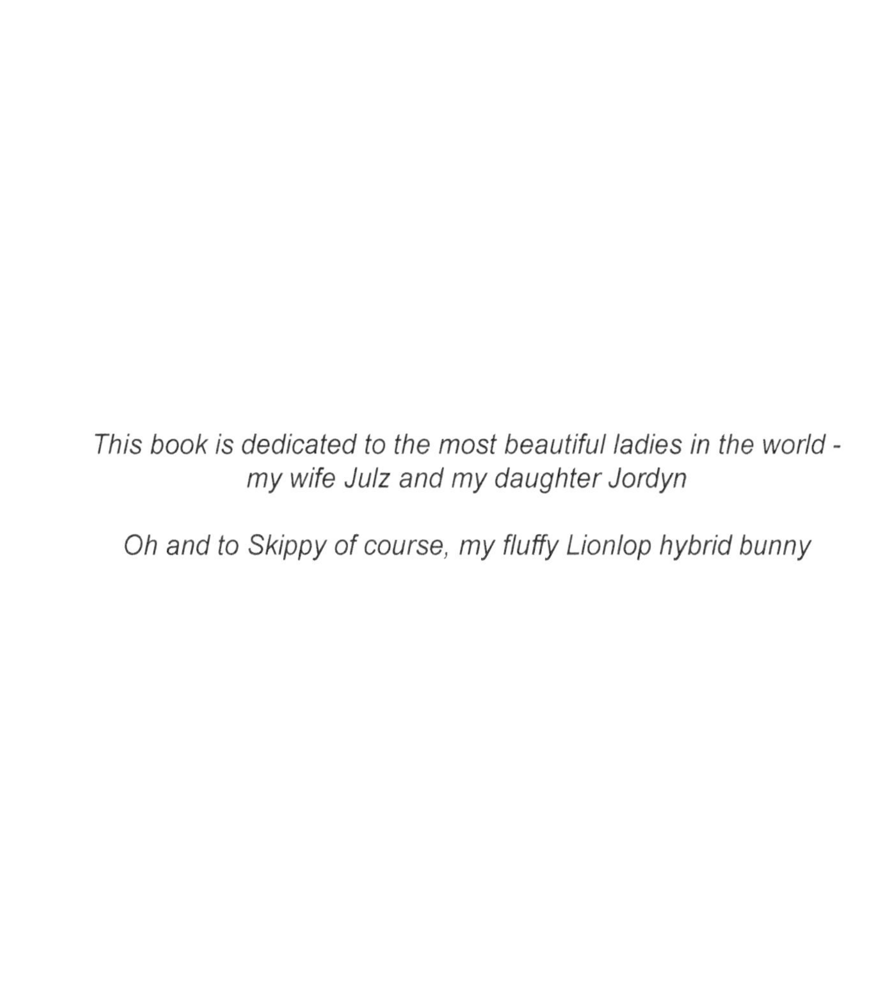

This book is dedicated to the most beautiful ladies in the world - my wife Julz and my daughter Jordyn

Oh and to Skippy of course, my fluffy Lionlop hybrid bunny

TABLE OF CONTENTS

- Indoor Setups
- Outdoor / Mixed Setups
- Essential Things to Buy

- Where to Get Your First Rabbit
- How to Pick a Rabbit
- Bringing Your Rabbit Home

- Principles of Feeding Your Rabbit
- Feeding Different Kinds of Food
- Feeding and Toilet Training Go Together

- Picking Up Your Rabbit
- Free-Roaming Time
- Grooming Your Rabbit

Why a Bunny?

A bunny, or, the domestic rabbit is one of the most popular pets in the world. While not as popular as dogs and cats, it's also an ideal pet especially for young people who want to learn about care and responsibility.

Before you decide to get a bunny or any pet, you need to think about it very carefully. Here are some things to consider. You should get a pet rabbit if you can put a check mark on each of these:

☑ You want a friendly pet that won't take up a lot of your time.

☑ You want a pet but you need one that doesn't make a lot of noise.

☑ You expect to take care of your pet for about 10 years.

- ☑ You want a clean pet that doesn't smell bad if taken cared of properly.

- ☑ You are considering to adopt a pet instead of buying one.

- ☑ You want a pet that can spend all of its time indoors.

☑ You can spend a few minutes a day to take care of the rabbit.

☑ You will love your pet even though it's not "cuddly" all the time.

☑ You will love your pet even though it won't travel or walk with you all the time.

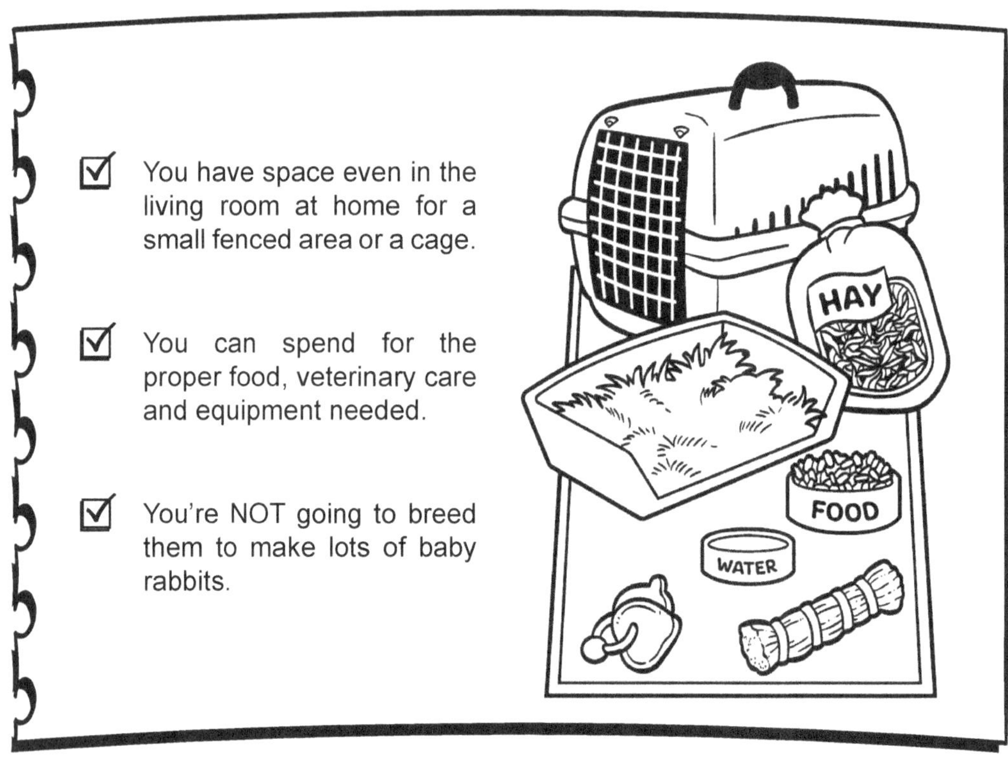

☑ You have space even in the living room at home for a small fenced area or a cage.

☑ You can spend for the proper food, veterinary care and equipment needed.

☑ You're NOT going to breed them to make lots of baby rabbits.

This seems like a long list, but I made this because I remember getting my first rabbits when I was 9 years old. I probably received more than 10 of them as gifts because my birthday was on the exact date of Easter Sunday that year. At first, I was happy but then after that, I realized that it was difficult to keep a lot of rabbits. Sadly, I had to give most of them away.

I learned two important lessons that time. First, that pets shouldn't be given as "surprise" gifts. Rather, pets should be wholehearted decisions for people who want them. Second, that a prospective pet owner should learn more before he/she buys a pet—and this book does just that for those who want rabbits as pets.

If you are making a wholehearted decision to be a rabbit owner and wish more to learn more, then this book is for you. In it you'll learn just about everything you need to take care of rabbits, including preparing a home for your first bunny and where to get it, feeding and living with it. Take this journey with me down our little burrow to having many years of happiness with your pet bunny!

TRIVIA! The word "bunny" also refers to rabbits, especially young ones. It comes from the term bun in the ancient Scottish language which means "tail of a hare."

Chapter 1
WHAT IS A RABBIT?

Pet rabbits or domestic rabbits bear the Latin scientific name *Oryctolagus cuniculus.* They are descended from the wild European rabbit.

For a very long time, rabbits were kept for their meat. It was only in recent times that they have become pets in many places in the world. This means that they are NOT wild animals but have lived with people just like dogs, cats, chickens, horses, cows and pigs.

Rabbits come from a group of mammals known as lagomorphs. This group also includes hares, jackrabbits and the pika. All animals from this group are herbivores, which means they eat only plant-based food. They are NOT rodents like rats and mice.

A special feature of the lagomorphs is that their teeth keep growing and need to be worn down through eating tough plant material in order to keep their teeth at the right length.

In the wild, the ancestors of the domestic rabbits lived by chewing on grass and other plants as much as they could. They were "prey animals" which meant they were hunted by predators like wolves and snakes. This is why rabbits are awake during early mornings (dawn) and early evenings (dusk) since these windows are the times when the predators are not very active.

Rabbits also developed powerful hind legs that help them run fast, instincts to dig up burrows, and a nervous personality that gets frightened easily. While this does not hold true anymore for the domestic rabbits today, understanding this helps pet owners know that while rabbits make great pets, they are more fragile than cats and dogs.

Rabbits are well-known for breeding very easily. This means that they multiply rapidly especially when there are no predators. In 1788, a group of Englishmen who settled in Australia brought with them some rabbits. Some of these escaped and, because there were no natural predators in the area, they multiplied rapidly.

Since they ate up farm crops, they were even considered as pests. This same mistake is committed by rabbit pet keepers too. This is why many pet shelters all over the world are filled with orphaned rabbits who need a home since pet owners did not expect their pets to multiply so fast in just a short amount of time.

Today, communities of rabbit pet keepers now discourage the breeding of rabbits but instead encourage people to adopt a rabbit from an animal shelter. The good news is that the various breeds are usually found in the shelters where they are brought for adoption.

Moreover, rabbit breeders serve an important role in the community as well as they tend to be specialists in their breed. This means that they study a particular breed or a few of them, and seek to raise healthy rabbits from this breed. This is also good, though expensive for budding bunny owners. There are also many shows where proud pet owners can enter their rabbits to compete in much the same way as dogs and cats do.

CHAPTER 2
BREEDS OF DOMESTIC RABBITS

Domestic rabbits now have over 50 breeds recognized all over the world. Depending on the breed, domestic rabbits have different sizes, color patterns, length, texture of their fur and even different shapes of ears (long, short, standing or lopped). While larger breeds tend to have shorter lives than smaller breeds, domestic rabbits usually have a lifespan of about 10 years.

Here are a few examples of the large breeds that are common and were once kept for their meat:

New Zealand

This is one of the most common breeds of rabbits found in pet stores. It comes in various colors and color combinations including white, red, brown and dark gray.

Dutch

The Dutch breed is one of the most recognizable color patterns found in a rabbit. While the word "Dutch" would usually mean the country Netherlands, this breed was actually perfected over many years in the United Kingdom.

Some other breeds have specialized fur:

Angora

The various types of Angora rabbit all have one thing in common: very, very long fur! They were bred this way since their fur is plucked and gathered and turned into Angora wool. As a pet, they are just a little bit more difficult to take care of since they have to be groomed more frequently.

Rex
This medium-sized rabbit is also bred for its fur. But unlike the Angora, it has short but very soft and velvety fur that makes it almost seem like a stuffed toy!

Lastly, the dwarf breeds which have become more popular lately:

Holland Lop
This breed from the Netherlands is quickly becoming one of the most popular breeds for rabbit keepers. It has long but laid down or "lopped" ears, a flat face and somewhat fluffy fur.

Lionhead

This breed is also very popular since it has a unique look from its propped up hair that looks like a lion's mane. Since it has long fur, it also needs more frequent grooming than most other breeds.

Netherland Dwarf

One of the smallest rabbit breeds, it is popular in rabbit shows since it tends to look like a kit even when it is an adult. It has short, propped up ears and an alert look.

There are also hybrids, which means these are rabbits that have different breed of parents. These rabbits tend to have the appearance or characteristics of both their parents.

In general, different breeds don't differ in care too much. Just follow the guidelines found in the next chapters and you'll have a healthy, happy companion for a long time.

CHAPTER 3
PREPARING A HOME
FOR YOUR RABBIT

To have a healthy, happy companion rabbit for a long time, pet owners can use the following guidelines.

Indoor Setups

Most people think that rabbits are best kept outdoors where they can run, play and eat natural grass. While it's true that this may be good in certain places, nowadays in most areas it is not recommended to do this because of the possible dangers a rabbit might encounter.

Some examples of these dangers include:

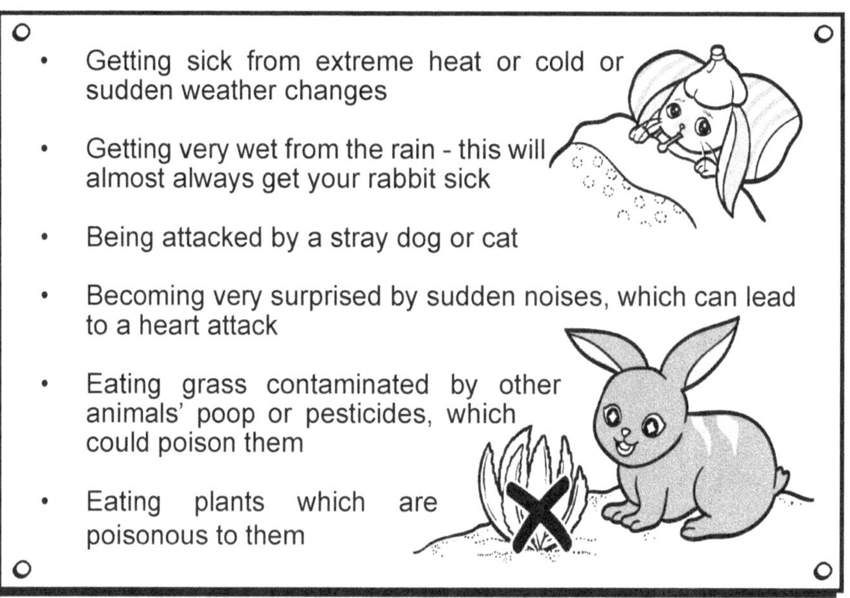

As mentioned in Chapter 1, rabbits are, by nature, prey animals. This means that they may tend to perceive any new things they encounter as dangers and react in a very nervous way. Whether it's a car horn, a birthday party next door or some construction work, pet owners cannot control what rabbits encounter outdoors. However, pet owners can easily control what their rabbits encounter indoors.

Here are some ideal setups indoors:

1. **A fenced area** - This is probably the simplest way to house a rabbit indoors. Those made for dogs called "puppy pens" and even those made for toddlers are ideal for this. Just make sure it has a height of at least 3 feet to make sure your pet won't jump over it.

2. **An indoor hutch** - While it saves more space, it does constrict your rabbit's space for a good amount of the day. This would require you to be very strict with your rabbit's free-roaming time (more on that in Chapter 6).

3. **A free-roaming room** - This is probably not feasible for most people as it's very difficult to allocate a whole room just for one rabbit. It also requires one to do more rabbit-proofing, which is difficult since a rabbit will just munch at anything including corners of walls and wires around them.

Rabbit-Proofing Your Home

Rabbit-proofing means you make your home and where the rabbit will be staying safe from danger to your pet and keeping it from damaging your stuff and your house. It's easy to do this for an indoor fence and a hutch, but a little harder for an entire room and probably near-impossible to completely do this for the entire house. This is why, as you'll be reading on in Chapter 6, free-roaming time should still be supervised by YOU or a responsible adult.

Some things to keep in mind to rabbit-proof your home:

- Keep wires out of their reach or cover them with wire covers or hoses.

- Keep away chemicals such as cleaning detergent, bleach, floor wax and soap out of their reach.

- Seal up electrical sockets within their reach with baby plugs.

- Cover legs and corners of the house.

This may seem like a lot of work, but if rabbits are supervised during their free-roaming time, then you do not have to completely do the list above. You can stop your rabbit by gently reprimanding it which will prevent any harm to your rabbit or your items at home. To learn how to do this, go to Chapter 7.

If you really insist on bringing your rabbit outside (despite some of the potential dangers that were mentioned), then here are some setups that you can try:

1. **Indoor / Outdoor mix** - you could keep your rabbit inside a hutch or a fenced area inside, then bring it out for free-roaming time within a larger fenced area in your garden or your fenced lawn, making sure that you have rabbit-proofed the area. Note that your rabbit WILL try to eat any plant so make sure that you keep plants you do not want your rabbit to munch or poisonous ones out of its reach.

2. **Fenced area with a hutch** - in this setup, your rabbit is staying completely outdoors. Make sure that there is a roofed portion away from direct sunlight or for them to run where they can easily retreat to. Many zoos tend to house their rabbits this way.

<u>**Essential Things To Buy**</u>

Aside from setting up their home, there are a few essential equipment and supplies you need to get before you bring your first rabbit home.

Hay and Hay Pellets
Hay specifically for rabbits (usually alfalfa for kittens and timothy for adults) and hay pellets will make up most of your rabbit's diet. Please note that there are pellets marketed as "rabbit pellets" but may contain a large percentage of corn, grain and other ingredients that are not hay. These are not ideal for rabbits over a long period of time. For both hay and hay pellets, make sure you have a steady source to get this from. Read more about feeding your rabbit in Chapter 5.

Hay Feeder
There are different types of contraptions that can be considered hay feeders. Some may be wooden boxes with a few holes while others are just wire trays that could be hung from a cage or fence. The important thing is that the feeder could be put in a corner of the fence or the hutch filled with hay, right next to the litter box. This is also essential for toilet training which is found in Chapter 5.

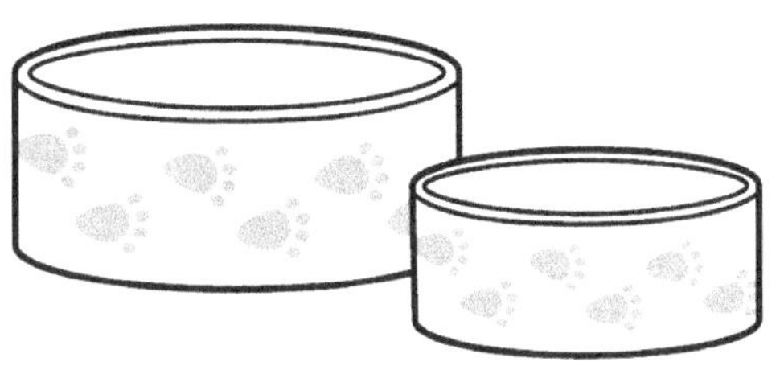

Food and Water Bowl
You would usually want two bowls, one for water and one for hay pellets. Make sure you get heavy ceramic bowls because otherwise, they will be thrown around like toys and may make a mess.

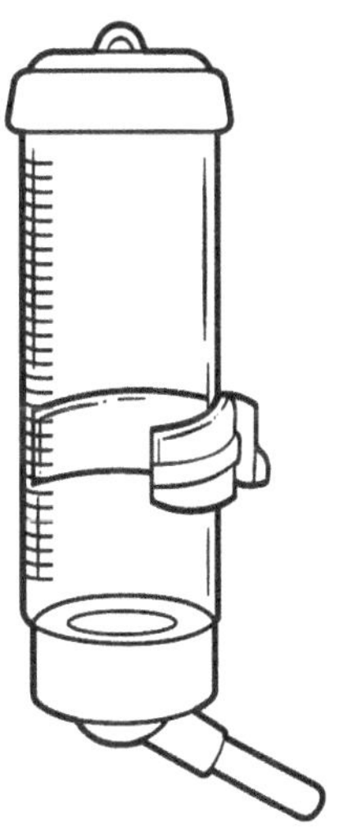

Drinking Bottle with Stopper
These can also be used for rabbits. However, bowls are more ideal since they drink water much easily via a bowl. For some people though, they like bottles because they are more convenient since they do not get dirty easily. There are various types and sizes of drinking bottles that can be attached to your hutch, cage or fence easily. Make sure you ask the pet store owner to get the right type and size for your rabbit (around 600ml) as the smallest ones are for hamsters and the biggest ones are for very large dogs!

Litter Box

Litter boxes are usually made for cats. However, many of these litter boxes may be a bit too high that your rabbit will have a hard time climbing in. Therefore, select a litter box that is lower like for short-legged cats. Even just a deep-dish or deep tray that your rabbit can fit itself in also works. DO NOT buy cat litter as you will be using hay for litter as well. DO stock up on old newspapers as they are ideal to line the bottom of the tray.

Grooming Comb

There are different types of combs you can use. The ones most used are the specialized combs for cats and small dogs. For as long as you can collect a rabbit's hair when it sheds without causing pain to the rabbit, then you have a good comb. You can even use ones meant for people!

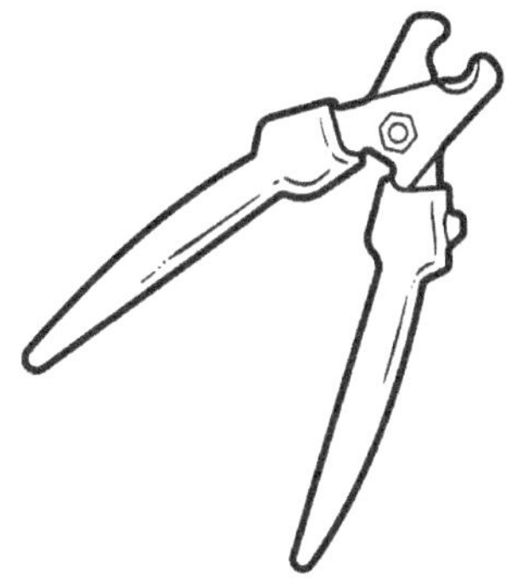

Nail Clipper

There is a specific type of nail clipper for small pet mammals. This is also the one used for cats. It is important to get a sharp, good quality one as a dull one will cause discomfort to your rabbit.

Carpet

A carpet is particularly useful for those that house their rabbits indoors in a fenced area. Slippery cemented or varnished wooden floors are not very comfortable for rabbits. Choose inexpensive carpets with short strands that will not tangle. Fancy carpets with long strands can potentially cause discomfort to your rabbit because they tend to snag on their nails.

Toys

Rabbits are extremely fond of toys. You do not need to buy pet rabbit toys specifically, as even cardboard boxes or old children's toys (that don't have harmful paint on them) would suffice. More examples of these are found in Chapter 6.

CHAPTER 4
ACQUIRING YOUR FIRST RABBIT

<u>**Where to Get Your First Rabbit**</u>

While most people think of a pet store when it comes to acquiring their first pet, there are actually other options. The three most common options are discussed here along with their "pros and cons." Pros mean that these are the advantages of that option while cons talk about their disadvantages.

OPTION #1: Adopt a rabbit

This is definitely the best option in terms of the cost and also helping out your community. To adopt a rabbit, you just need to visit your local animal shelter and pick out a rabbit that you like. It helps the community because these rabbits need a home and the ones in shelters were usually abandoned by their previous owners. Some pros and cons of this option are:

PROS
- The adoption fee is not very expensive.
- You help out your local community by giving an orphaned rabbit a home.
- Usually, shelter rabbits have already been spayed or neutered (to learn about what this means, go to Chapter 7).

CONS
- It's not as easy to get the age breed, color or sex that you might prefer.

OPTION #2 - Buy directly from a breeder

This option is the usual option of people who are thinking about joining a rabbit show or have a particular breed, color and sex that they want. Breeders, especially reputable ones, are very careful about breeding their rabbits. They make sure that they get the qualities they want in the rabbits they breed.

PROS
- You can easily get young rabbits and the breed, color and sex that you want.
- You get papers that certify that tell you information about the rabbits.
- Breeders can tell you the history of the rabbit they have, making sure you know everything you need to know about your new pet before taking it home.

CONS
- This is usually the most expensive option.
- Breeders are not always found nearby your location.

OPTION #3 - Buy from a pet store

This option is probably the most common, but is by far not really the most ideal in most cases. Some pet stores tend to sell rabbits in which the breed, source and the conditions in which they were bred can be unclear. Unlike the other two options, you do not always have an expert like a vet or a breeder who is very knowledgeable in caring about rabbits. While there are good pet stores (such as those that get from breeders), it's usually better to adopt or get from a breeder.

PROS
* Not as expensive as getting from a breeder, but more expensive than adoption (especially when you include the cost of spaying or neutering a rabbit).
* Easy to find pet stores that sell rabbits - chances are there are a few where you live.

CONS
* You do not get expert advice when you buy a rabbit.
* Since it's hard to determine the sex of a rabbit when it is young, pet stores tend to make mistakes in identifying the sex of their rabbits as well.
* Often times, the important facts about the rabbit such as where it came from and the like are unclear.

How to Pick a Rabbit

Whether it be at the shelter, a breeder or the pet store, you will have the choice of which rabbit to pick among available ones. The size, breed, color and the kind of fur that they have are all up to what you want. What you need to pay attention to are:

1. **The rabbit's behavior** - since you are keeping one as a pet, do check for one that is alert but not too nervous when you go near it. When you call it, check to see if it's curious about you or very relaxed, not one that will bolt away in fear.

2. **The rabbit's age** - rabbits under the age of 8 weeks should not be considered for pet keeping. This is because rabbits younger than 8 weeks are still drinking milk from their mothers and their tummies may have trouble eating hay and hay pellets. The ideal time to get a kitten is between 8-12 weeks, but even older than that to up to two years should make ideal pets.

3. **The rabbit's cleanliness** - rabbits are very clean pets. They clean themselves regularly. When they are extremely dirty especially in the vent area (where their poop comes out) it may be a sign of sickness. For more about a rabbit's grooming behavior, go to Chapter 6.

4. **The rabbit's shape** - rabbits should not be overly thin nor very fat. A thin rabbit looks like its bones are seen through the skin, and a sign of sickness if it does not want to eat the food given to it. On the other hand, a rabbit that is too fat is probably not being given the proper diet. Usually, fat rabbits are fed lots of foods like carrots, fruit or non-hay pellets—all of which can be bad for the rabbit.

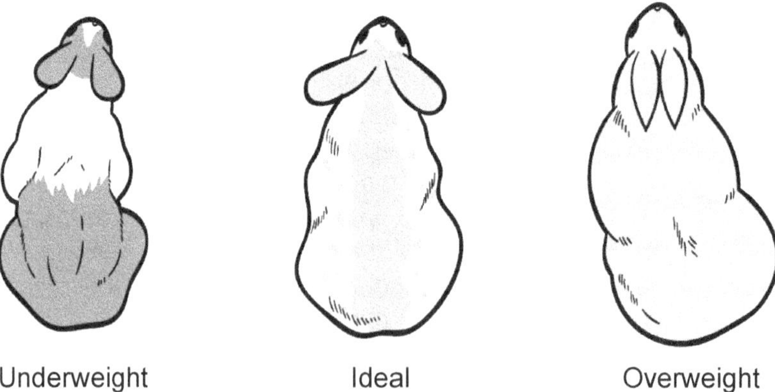

Underweight   Ideal   Overweight

Bringing Your Rabbit Home

A rabbit can be brought home in a container that is safe for it. Some examples include a small pet carrier or even a cardboard box with a lot of holes. You would also want a small amount of hay in there from where it came from to help it feel more safe and familiar with its surroundings.

Normally, when you bring a rabbit home, it will feel a lot more nervous since it was moved from its home to yours. This is why preparing its home in Chapter 3 is so important before actually getting the rabbit for it to avoid any confusion and help it adjust quickly to its new home.

For the first week, it's important to let your rabbit know first that the new surroundings are safe. While it's best not to bother it or attempt to carry it immediately, it is not bad to offer your hand to pet it or to see if it will take food from your hand. For the first week, focus on feeding routines found in the next chapter of the book and as for building a friendship with your newfound friend, go to Chapter 6.

CHAPTER 5
FEEDING YOUR RABBIT

<u>**Principles of Feeding Your Rabbit**</u>

The topic of what proper food to feed rabbits tends to differ from one expert keeper to the next. The general idea of what is good to feed a rabbit has also changed since the type of food given to raising rabbits for meat was meant for fattening them up.

Today, here are some feeding guidelines to follow that are agreed upon by many expert keepers and rabbit vets:

1. Most or about 80% of a rabbit's diet must be composed of very fibrous plant material such as hay or grass.

2. A rabbit's diet must be supplemented by food that is balanced with vitamins and minerals.

3. Fresh dark green leafy green vegetables may be given up to 1 cup everyday.

4. Root crops and fruits are given only every once in a while as treats.

TRIVIA! Herbivores have specialized stomachs that allow them to digest the tough plant *cellulose* into energy. Human stomachs cannot do that so we usually just get vitamins and minerals from our leafy vegetables as well as the roughage that helps our digestion.

Feeding Different Kinds of Food

Hay

In the wild, rabbits will have fresh grass to eat all the time. However, that is almost always very unsafe today. While many types of grass found outside are safe for rabbits, even weeds and flowers like dandelion, the problem is that grass outside could contain harmful things like pesticides and parasites for your rabbit that could kill it. Pesticides refer to chemicals used to kill insect pests such as grasshoppers and caterpillars while parasites refer to various types of organisms such as pinworms and stomach worms that will live off your rabbit and make it sick or even kill it.

Therefore, it is best to give it hay. Thankfully, hay for rabbits is usually easy to find, not very expensive and there are many good quality ones. Here are a few different kinds:

1. **Timothy Hay** - This type of hay is the most common to feed your rabbit. It is available in 1st, 2nd or 3rd cut as indicated by the packaging. 1st and 2nd cut hay are ideal for adult rabbits while 3rd cut hay would be ideal for kittens up to 6 months old. It also has a very sweet smell. Feeding your rabbit Timothy Hay throughout its lifetime is okay.

2. **Alfalfa Hay** - This type of hay should only be fed to kittens up to 6 months old as it has a lower fiber content while having a high protein content.

3. **Meadow Hay** - This type of hay is a mixture of various types of hay and can even have dried flowers at times. It's good to feed this every once in a while to add variety to your rabbit's food.

TRIVIA! It was found that a suitable staple alternative for rabbits is fresh banana leaves. A study by two vets in India, namely Dr. Rohilla and Dr. Bujarbaruah, found that up to 40% diet of fresh banana leaves is acceptable for rabbits as the banana leaves contain 20% fiber content. If you live in places such as in Southeast Asia where fresh, pesticide-free banana leaves are easily obtainable, just wash the leaves with water, cut them into small strips then mix this with hay to feed your rabbit.

Water

While hay is the best food for your rabbits, it's also important to give them clean water all the time and an amount of hay pellets everyday.

Water is either placed in a bowl or in a drinking bottle with a metal ball stopper. Rabbits can easily drink from a ceramic bowl, but if it gets dirty, it needs to be replaced immediately. Rabbits have a harder time drinking from a bottle with a metal ball stopper, but it is more convenient. Either way, the water should be changed everyday and always be available to your rabbit.

Hay Pellet

Feed your rabbit ⅛ to ¼ cup of hay pellets everyday depending on the size of your rabbit. The reason why pellets are important is that pellets are fortified with vitamins and minerals like calcium that rabbits will not get as easily from just eating pure hay.

It's very important that when you feed hay pellets that you check the label to make sure the pellets are at least 18% fiber, though the best would be between 20-25%. Avoid pet food labeled as "for rabbits" or "rabbit pellets" that contain grain, oat, wheat or corn. These could make your rabbit gain too much weight or make it sick.

Fresh Dark Green Leafy Vegetables

These fresh dark green leafy vegetables are important to your rabbit's diet as vegetables provide your pet with additional vitamins and minerals, moisture and also variety which helps keep your bunny happy.

You do not have to feed these everyday, though it's good to give these at least 5 times a week. Measure about 1 cup per day and that would be the maximum for your pet as it needs to consume hay more than these vegetables.

Examples of good vegetables to feed your rabbit include Romaine lettuce, carrot tops, kale, arugula, mint, basil, cilantro, bok choy, watercress and dill.

Root Crops and Fruits

These types of food should be given to your rabbit only once in a while, and only after the first month of getting it used to eating its proper diet of hay, hay pellets and leafy greens which are actually "treats" for your rabbit. As a result, it can want this more and more though it's bad for it just as how lots of chocolate and candy are also bad for you.

Give only an adult's thumb size piece not more than twice a week. Examples of these treats include carrots, apples, papayas, mangoes and raisins.

FINAL NOTE ON FEEDING: Most common illnesses that rabbits tend to have as pets can be attributed to wrong feeding. Make sure to follow the above guidelines and you will have a healthy pet for years to come.

<u>**Feeding and Toilet Training Go Together**</u>

Back when they were wild European rabbits, they basically fed bit by bit the entire day mostly on grass and other plants they could find. They might have occasionally found fruits or root crops to eat, but this did not happen very often. Moreover, they concentrated their feeding habits mainly during the early morning and early evening (dusk and dawn) to avoid predators who were good at hunting in complete light and complete darkness.

In addition, rabbits avoided predators by pooping where they ate. This worked because predators would look for their droppings and assume that the rabbits would just be nearby. But since their droppings were dry and pretty much odorless with a little bit of their fur, predators who went to their area were actually misled since the rabbits would be home in their burrows by the time the predators got to their droppings!

Using the previous information, you will find that toilet training rabbits is actually quite simple. You simply need to set it up correctly:

1. Put the litter box in one corner of the hutch or fence.
2. Line newspapers inside the litter box and fill it with hay.
3. Put the hay feeder right next to the litter box.
4. Change the hay and the newspapers every 2-3 days.
5. Make sure there is always hay available for your rabbit.

If you make your setup like this as soon as your rabbit is first home, it will probably only take a few days to litter train your rabbit. This makes use of its instinct to poop where they eat and they will also mark it with their scent glands to remember to always pee and poop in the litter box.

One other plus to rabbits, especially ones fed on just hay and hay pellets, is that they produce dry little poop that look like larger peppercorns with a bit of hair. They are easily swept up or even picked up. Almost all of it will be left on the litter box.

CHAPTER 6
LIVING WITH YOUR RABBIT

Now that you have your rabbit in a suitable home and is feeding well, it's time to look at the other things that would help your rabbit be happier and healthier while at the same time building a relationship with you.

Picking Up Your Rabbit

Properly Picking Up Your Rabbit

As mentioned, rabbits are prey animals. In the wild, anything that picks them up is probably bound to eat them. This is why picking up rabbits is not as easy as picking up dogs and cats. But with a little bit of practice and your rabbit learning to trust you, you should be able to do this without scaring your rabbit. You can even get to a point that a rabbit likes getting picked up because it means it will get stroked and cuddled which it tends to like as well.

Before attempting to pick up your rabbit, make sure that it is used to you already. This means that at least several days have gone by in a feeding routine with your new pet. Call it by its name in a gentle voice (Example: "Hey Skippy! How are you today?") and be consistent in what you do daily with your rabbit. When you see your rabbit is not nervous seeing you and is used to you, do try to pick it up.

While there are several methods that rabbit keepers like to use to pick up a rabbit, this book will discuss the simplest and easiest one:

Step 1: Indian sit right next to your rabbit.

Step 2: Pet and stroke your rabbit first and make sure it feels safe with you.

Step 3: Gently move the rabbit in which it is sideways in front of you and its butt is in the direction of your dominant hand.

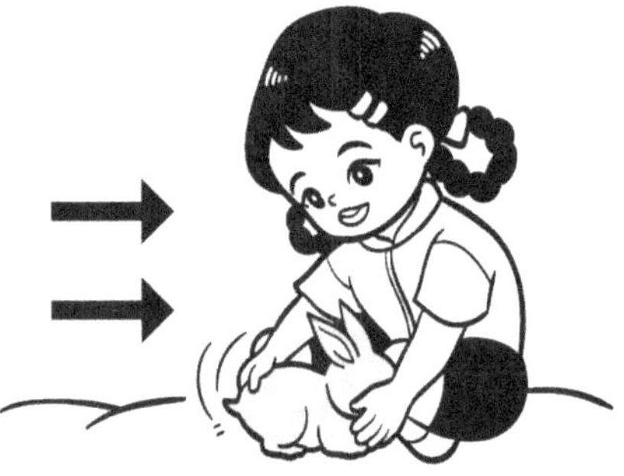

Step 4: Gently reach to the other side of the rabbit and gently push it towards you using your dominant hand.

Step 5: While your dominant hand is on one side of the rabbit, gently push your other hand from the front of the rabbit underneath it.

Step 6: Put the rabbit close to you with a firm hold enough that it will not be able to struggle but not too firm as to cause the rabbit any discomfort.

Step 7: Stroke your rabbit and reassure it in a gentle voice (Example: "Hey there, Skippy. It's okay.. It's okay…").

If you do this correctly, your dominant arm should be along the side of the rabbit and able to stroke and pet its head. Your non-dominant arm is underneath the rabbit. The other side of the rabbit should be on your chest area.

When your rabbit does agree to be picked up, you can also reward it by cuddling with it by gently stroking and patting it and even giving it a treat. It will teach your rabbit that getting picked up is a good thing and that it can trust you.

Things to Avoid When Picking Up Your Rabbit

Remember that rabbits are prey animals that easily get nervous from getting picked up. Therefore, do not make jerking movements when picking it up like grabbing it with one hand. There are also ways by which picking up the rabbit would cause it pain. For example, do not pick up the rabbit using its ears, skin or fur.

If you are trying to pick up your rabbit and it goes away from you, give it a bit more time. If you are in a hurry (like if you have an appointment with the vet), use a treat and lead it into a pet carrier or a small cardboard box with holes.

Rabbits also need their daily exercise. Thankfully, this is not so hard to do. As mentioned earlier, rabbits are most active early in the morning as well as early in the evening and kind of just rest in between those two time periods. This is very convenient for pet owners who are children that go to school or even adults that go to work.

When you get up in the morning, just let your rabbit out of the fence or hutch and let it roam freely in your fairly rabbit-proofed environment (you can review this back in Chapter 3). This needs to be just around 15-30 minutes. After your pet's free-roaming time, put it back in its fence or hutch.

Do this again late in the afternoon. While your rabbit is roaming, just keep an eye out for it. You can still take a bath, brush your teeth or do your homework during this time.

This routine helps your rabbit understand its own routine, get some exercise and satisfy its natural urge to explore. This also teaches your pet that you are its owner and you are safe to be around with. In addition, it's very enjoyable to watch your rabbit during free-roaming time.

Toys for Your Rabbit

It is also ideal to place toys inside the hutch, fence or even the free-roaming area of your rabbit. These keep your rabbit busy and active. It's also quite fun to watch a rabbit toss things around, chew them up and just have fun with objects. Old stuffed toys, cardboard boxes, old toilet paper rolls, rattles and other baby-safe toys are all suitable for your rabbit for as long as they do not swallow any plaything.

It is indeed fun to watch and interact with your pet rabbit. Over a long time of bonding, you will naturally learn many of your pet's behaviors and what they mean. Of course, every rabbit is different and will have many differences with other rabbits. It's your job as the pet owner to really get to know your bunny. With that said, here are a few common behaviors of rabbits and what they mean:

Signs of Happiness

These three behaviors will be observed when your rabbit is excited and happy. This usually happens right at the start of free-roaming time when a rabbit knows that it will be given the chance to explore its surroundings once again. Bolting is when a rabbit runs around, sometimes in circles around you, objects and even other rabbits. A binky is when it jumps straight up. Falling over looks like a dog "playing dead" as it is when your rabbit falls quickly on its side.

Signs of Exploring

These are natural behaviors that show that your rabbit is exploring its place. All of these are good signs that your rabbit is healthy and happy. In the wild, they will dig around to make burrows or find food. Thus, your rabbit will "dig" indoors by scratching carpet or clothes left on the floor. Periscoping is an action when rabbits stand on their hind legs to be able to see higher. They also do this when they beg for food. Chinning is a way by which they mark their territory by rubbing their chins on something. This includes toys, their cage, ordinary objects and even people.

Signs of Affection

Rabbits, especially ones that have learned to trust and bond with you, will tend to be affectionate towards you. Like dogs, rabbits will lick you when they show their affection. This is actually social grooming for them, and they will bow afterwards to allow you to groom them. When this happens, gently stroke them to show that you are buddies. During this time, they tend to make noises that sound like a pig's "oink." This means that they are very relaxed and happy at the same time.

Signs of Stress

Rabbits will grunt at you, which sound like sudden snoring sounds when they feel as if they are being bothered. This will tend to happen when you try to pick them up but they are not in the mood or when they are not yet familiar with you. They may also kick their hind legs at you, as if to "kick dirt" in your face. If they are really bothered, they may even lunge at you. They do this with other rabbits to establish their territory. Do note that these types of behavior can be lessened if you have your rabbit neutered. This is discussed in Chapter 7.

For the most part, rabbits are very clean animals that do not need your help in grooming them. For one thing, you should NEVER give them a bath - this interferes with their body temperature and could get them sick easily.

Also, perhaps the cutest thing they do is actually when they groom themselves— they basically sit on their hind legs and start licking their hands and wiping their face. They do these fairly frequently, too!

There are two areas though that you could help them with, one is with brushing their fur and the other is in clipping their nails.

Brushing Fur

To brush your rabbit's fur, simply take a small comb or a pet comb and gently run it across your rabbit going in a direction away from its body. This can be done anytime especially when your rabbit has long fur which tends to get tangled. However, your rabbit would most appreciate this during its shedding period, which it tends to do several times a year.

You would know shedding when you see a lot of fur around the rabbit's hutch or cage. Brushing your pet helps a lot during this time because a bunny tends to swallow its fur when it grooms itself, which is not harmful but can cause discomfort.

By brushing your pet, you reduce the chance that swallowing fur happens. Sometimes, during brushing, you create a ball of fur that can be a bit larger than your rabbit!

Clipping Nails

In the wild, long nails keep a rabbit able to do essential things like digging and having a good grip on the grassy soil. For domestic rabbits kept indoors, long nails tend to snag on the carpet, break on the concrete or even scratch their owners.

Clipping nails is probably the most difficult task in your routine in keeping a rabbit because it is a skill that needs to be developed. It's best to do this with young kittens so that when they grow up, they are already used to it. When starting out, it's best to have an experienced adult, rabbit keeper or vet show you how it is done. When you are experienced, it's still best to have another person help you do this. Here's how to clip your rabbit's nails:

Step 1: Pick the rabbit up properly (look for the steps early in this chapter).

Step 2: Put it on a table right next to you, stroke it and make it feel safe.

Step 3: Put your dominant hand on the rabbit's butt while the other hand is underneath it.

Step 4: Quickly but gently, flip the rabbit on its back on the table.

Step 5: Hold it firmly and keep whispering to it to let it know it's safe.

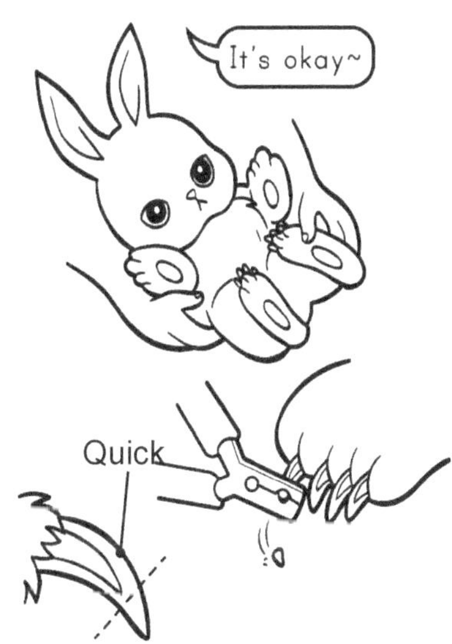

Step 6: Have an adult clip each nail using the pet nail clipper, being careful only to get the VERY MOST TIP of the five nails on each front paw and four nails on each of its hind paws.

Step 6 is particularly important as overcutting can cause pain and a bit of bleeding to your rabbit. While this is not particularly dangerous for your pet, it will hurt it and it will feel less safe the next time it gets a nail trimming. Thankfully, you only need to clip your rabbit's nails about once a month.

A Summary of Everything You Need to Do with Your Rabbit

Daily Things to Do
☑ Replace water.
☑ Give rabbit free roaming time.
☑ Stroke & say hello to your rabbit.

Every Other Day Things to Do
☑ Give some dark green leafy green vegetables.
☑ Replace hay in the feeder and litter box.

Weekly Things to Do
☑ Give a "treat" like soft vegetables, carrots and fruits.
☑ Check if its vent is clean.
☑ Brush your rabbit's fur.

Monthly things to do
☑ Clip your rabbit's nails.

Periodical Things to Do
☑ Veterinary check up (immediate if rabbit is sick).
☑ Have your rabbit neutered (once per lifetime).
☑ Groom if it is shedding.

CHAPTER 7
YOUR RABBIT'S HEALTH

Bringing your rabbit to the pet doctor or veterinarian (or vet for short) is important. There are more reasons to bring your rabbit to the vet than only when it gets sick. In general, you can take the rabbit to the vet around twice a year just to check if it's healthy.

Just like humans, regular checkups make sure that your rabbit is in the best health it could be. In looking for a vet, make sure it is someone who specializes in rabbits. Here are some of the important things to do when you visit your vet.

<u>**Getting Your Rabbit Neutered**</u>

If your rabbit is not neutered yet, your rabbit will have behaviors that would make it very tough to keep. It will tend to mark its scent around the house, chase other rabbits, not be as easily trainable or worse, if kept with other rabbits and unknown to its owner, a female rabbit can get pregnant.

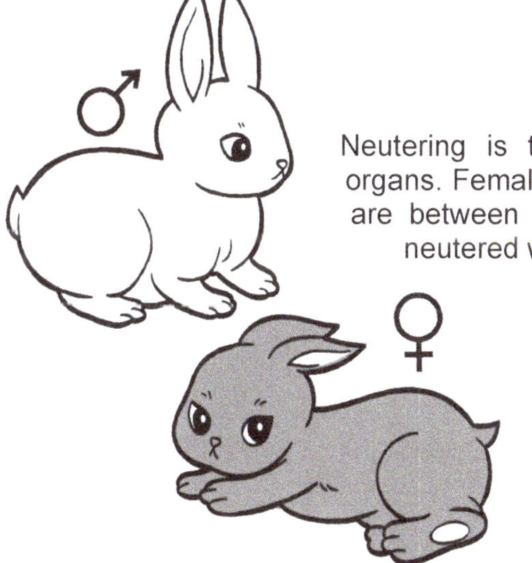

Neutering is the removal of a rabbit's reproductive organs. Female rabbits are neutered usually when they are between 4-6 months old while male rabbits are neutered when they are between 2-4 months old.

A vet performs the neutering procedure which is generally not very painful for your pet. The vet also decides whether the rabbit is okay to be neutered given its age and its current health condition.

The most important thing to remember is this: neutered pet rabbits make the best pet rabbits!

<u>**Getting Your Rabbit Vaccinated**</u>

People and many types of pets get vaccinated. Rabbits have vaccines too, but they tend to be different from place to place. A vaccine is a substance given to your rabbit (either made to swallow or injected by the vet) to protect it from a specific type of disease. Because of this, some places do not have rabbit vaccines because the disease does not exist in that area.

To find out the right type of vaccination for your rabbit, visit your local vet.

How to Tell If Your Rabbit is Sick

Just like people, rabbits can get sick, too. Improper diet, viruses, bacteria, parasites and so many other things can cause sickness. Some signs that your rabbit is sick are:

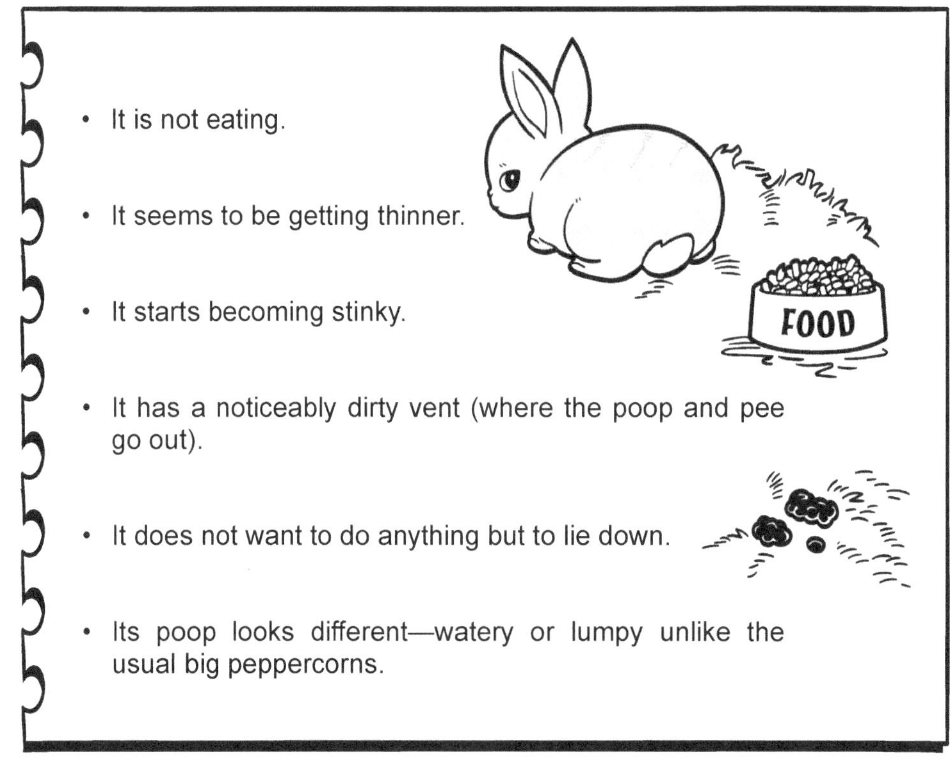

- It is not eating.

- It seems to be getting thinner.

- It starts becoming stinky.

- It has a noticeably dirty vent (where the poop and pee go out).

- It does not want to do anything but to lie down.

- Its poop looks different—watery or lumpy unlike the usual big peppercorns.

When you see these things, bring your rabbit to the vet immediately and follow all the directions that your vet tells you to do.

How to Tell When a Rabbit is Injured

Unlike a sickness, an injury happens when an accident happens to your rabbit. This often means that they are wounded or they bumped a leg. When you see your rabbit bleeding or limping, do the following first aid steps with the assistance of an adult:

- Have an adult gently hold down/ restrain the rabbit.

- For a wound - Take a piece of cotton gauze pad and place it on the area of the wound then wrap it with medical tape.

- For a limp - simply wrap the rabbit snugly in a clean towel.

- Place your rabbit carefully in the pet carrier and travel straight to the vet or animal hospital.

Remember that this first aid is only temporary. The real treatment comes from a vet. Often times, the vet may prescribe antibiotics, perform x-rays or even confine your rabbit to make sure that your rabbit gets better.

<u>**When the Inevitable Happens**</u>

Rabbits usually live about 10 years, but oftentimes an unexpected death of your pet can happen before that period. When this occurs, it can feel like losing a family member. This intense feeling of sadness is part of the process of grieving and is a part of your life as a pet owner.

Give your bunny the respect it deserves by burying it properly in a proper place like in the middle of your garden. Gather all other family members and remember the good times you had with your bunny. If you do not have a garden, call the disposal officer in your community to know how to dispose of your pet's body, in order not to spread any sicknesses around.

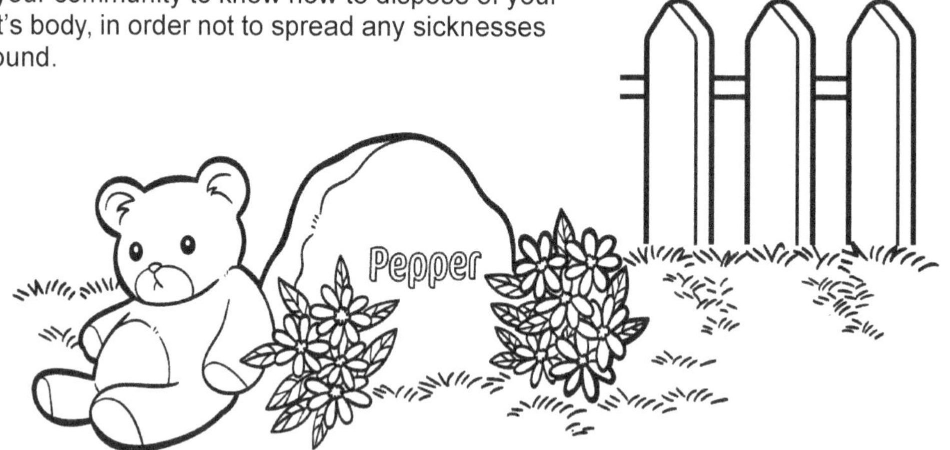

CHAPTER 8
CARING FOR A PREGNANT RABBIT

As mentioned, it is highly discouraged to breed your rabbits. This chapter is written more for those that "accidentally" breed one's own rabbits. But if you need more reasons why not to breed your rabbits, here are a few more:

- Having many rabbit kittens (the number is usually between 2 and 10) means that you will need to find homes for all these new rabbits. This is very difficult—all the orphaned rabbits in the animal shelters are proof of this.

- Does (female rabbits) have to be in perfect health or else they could suffer from complications and even die after giving birth to the kittens. The bad thing about this is that the kittens also die since they do not have a mother to nurse milk from.

- A doe can sometimes have a sort of "panic" mode that is not very well understood yet. When this happens, she will kill her own kittens.

Determining Whether a Rabbit is Pregnant or Not

As a good rabbit keeper, you may already have a schedule to bring your doe to the vet to have it neutered. However, you start noticing your doe's tummy has gotten bigger. The thing is, does can already get pregnant when put with male rabbits even when they are as young as 3 months old! However, the safest pregnancies for does usually occur when they are 7-8 months old and it gets somewhat unsafe after that.

When this happens, bring your doe to the vet to confirm if she really is pregnant.

Here are some other signs that may show your rabbit is pregnant:

- She displays nesting behavior by lining her hutch or fence with fur.

- She starts becoming aggressive towards the bucks (male rabbits) around her and may even hurt them.

- She starts behaving differently even towards you in various ways like not minding you and not eating at all then suddenly eating too much.

<u>**What to Do If a Rabbit is Pregnant**</u>

There are several things you must do to make sure your doe has the highest chance of having a successful pregnancy, that is, she gives birth to live kittens safely:

1. Separate her fence or hutch from other rabbits. However, keep them in a general area as she may get distressed if she does not see her mate or friends.

2. Put a soft covered space that she can easily go in and out of to build her nest. An example of this would be a cat litter box with a cover. She will line this with her fur to keep the kittens warm.

3. Feed her alfalfa hay (the variety usually given to baby rabbits back in Chapter 5). This is better for her since she needs the higher protein content of this hay to develop her babies.

4. Wait for a few weeks, as it only takes about 1 month from her pregnancy until she gives birth.

<u>**What to Do When a Rabbit Gives Birth**</u>

Hopefully, your rabbit gives birth to a healthy litter of kittens. When this happens, leave the mother alone to nurse her kittens. DO NOT put other rabbits back with her in as she can immediately get pregnant again.

At about 8 weeks old, bring the kits to the vet to determine the sex of each bunny. At this age, it is hard for you to determine whether they are boys or girls, but they need to be separated to avoid another pregnancy.

Hopefully, you can find good homes for every single kitten. If you cannot do so, contact your local animal shelter to house the kits. In addition, have your rabbits neutered as soon as you can.

Every Bunny Deserves a Good Home

After you, the reader, have read this book, the hope is that you not only will be a happy pet owner because of a cute rabbit, but also a responsible one.

Fact is, rabbits nowadays need good and responsible pet owners for their own good. Sadly, many shelters are overcrowded with more rabbits as time goes by because many people do not know about good rabbit keeping practices nor do they know where to find other experienced rabbit keepers.

With that said, it is a guarantee that in following the guidelines of this book, that you will become a more competent rabbit keeper and have many more happy years with your bunny.

Happy Bunny Keeping!

Frequently Asked Questions (FAQs)

Q Can I keep more than one rabbit at a time?

A Yes, you can. Rabbits can actually live together in a single fenced area and the instructions in the book will also apply to more than one rabbit. However, do make sure they are neutered so that they do not have undesirable behaviors such as breeding and fighting over their territory.

Q I saw my rabbit eating its own poop. Is this okay?

A Yes. Oftentimes, herbivores do this because they need to obtain all the goodness of the food that they cannot do in one digestion. Thus, they eat it again.

 Can you train rabbits to do tricks?

 Yes, however, that is not covered in this book. It's also not as simple as training dogs. The simplest trick would be to train your rabbits to beg. When your rabbits show a behavior you like such as periscoping or circling, give them a treat. This will increase the chances that they will do this in order to get a treat from you. Rabbits though can learn to jump through hoops, perform elaborate tricks and other amazing things. If you want to learn how to do this, approach rabbit pet keepers or even your local zoo or petting zoo for the right information.

 Can my rabbit live with other animals?

 Yes, for as long as your other pets are gentle and, ideally, live apart. Remember that rabbits are prey animals and they may be frightened by a very excited dog or cat.

 I experience bites and scratches from my rabbit. What do I do?

 Scratches are easily avoided if you groom your rabbit well as mentioned in Chapter 6. As for bites, rabbits may lightly bite (called a "nip") to get your attention, but it's actually quite rare for rabbits to really bite aggressively. To solve this issue, simply continue to bond with them as suggested in Chapter 6 and it should be resolved. Sometimes as well, this happens when a rabbit is always free-roaming and never inside a fence or a hutch. This makes it feel that it is "the boss," which indicates that it is not advisable to continue in your pet owner to pet relationship. Establish a routine as recommended in Chapter 6 with the rabbit inside a hutch or fence most of the day and only a bit of free-roaming time. Wear gloves as you do this to avoid getting bitten.

Bibliography

P.P. Rohilla & K.M. Bujarbaruah (2000). Effect of banana leaves feeding on growth of rabbits. Indian Veterinary Journal. 77, 902-903.

Hirschhorn, Howard (1991). All About Rabbits. TFN Publications, Inc.

Acknowledgments

To my parents, Allan and Elnor, for always supporting me in my hobbies growing up, even when it involved strange smells and living creatures swarming the home.

To my Uncle Ferdinand who encouraged to breed rabbits with me when I was much younger—opening up possibilities such as the breeds of rabbit not found in the pet store.

To my Uncle Florante who is the other rabbit enthusiast in the family, and, frankly the better one.

To the Catabijan family and the Saint Matthew's Publishing Corporation and Kahel Press staff, for once again for putting their trust in me and the fact that, yes, I've kept not just a lot of aquariums but a lot of rabbits as well.

To the Philippine community of rabbit keepers, breeders and the exotic pet veterinarians who keep this hobby thriving and ethical.

To my wife, Julz, and my wonderful in-laws for always supporting me and encouraging me in my endeavors such as this.

To my daughter, Jordyn, and my rabbit, Skippy, for providing the inspiration for the cover of this book.

Most of all, to Jesus who saved me by His grace and allowed me the privilege to do so many things. I do this in His name.

Thank you.

About the Author

Fiel John Meria is a happy husband to Julz and a huggable father to Jordyn Ysabelle.

He has kept various types of animals growing up to the point that he could have probably started a zoo at some point. For now, he is content to have his 12 exotic goldfish and Skippy—his dwarf Holland Lop / Lionhead hybrid bunny.

He is the Director of Project Pond (People Overcoming Neurodevelopmental Difficulties) where he life coaches, travels and does quirky projects with people who have Attention-Deficit Hyperactivity Disorder, Autism Spectrum Disorder, and Specific Learning Disabilities. He and his wife Julz are both diagnosed with ADHD and dedicate themselves to sharing the love of Jesus to families who have children and members with special needs.